The

NEST

EGG MYTH

How To Build Wealth And Happiness
Outside Of The Traditional System

By

Prof. John S. Mathis

DISCLAIMER

Copyright © 2024 by John S. Mathis

CONTENTS

Description

Are you aspiring to attain amazing economic independence and manifest the life of your dreams? Do you think that saving money for retirement is the greatest approach to protecting your future? Do you feel frustrated and perplexed by the complex and turbulent financial system?

If you responded affirmatively to any of these inquiries, then you must delve into the content of this book. In this book, John S. Mathis exposes the reality behind the nest egg myth, and why it is a dangerous and outdated strategy for wealth generation. He also shows you how to develop wealth and happiness outside of the traditional system, using the four pillars of wealth: income, assets, attitude, and lifestyle.

You will learn how to create multiple streams of passive income without working more, how to overcome fear, scarcity, and limiting beliefs that hold you back from achieving your financial goals, how to plan, execute, and monitor your wealth strategy, how to develop the skills, knowledge, and discipline to achieve financial freedom, how to enjoy your money and live a fulfilling life, and how to protect, grow, and share your wealth with future generations.

This book is not a get-rich-quick system, nor a one-size-fits-all answer. It is a practical and proven strategy that can help you generate wealth and happiness on your terms, based on your unique values, vision, and purpose. Whether you are just starting out, or already have some wealth, this book will help you take your financial game to the next level.

Don't let the nest egg fallacy restrict you from living your greatest life. Get this book today and start building money and pleasure outside of the traditional system. Kindly click on the "**buy button**" to own this now!

Introduction

In a society where financial security is often equated with the notion of a well-preserved "nest egg," we find ourselves standing at the edge of a fundamental paradigm change in personal finance. This book, "The Nest Egg Myth: How to Build Wealth and Happiness Outside of the Traditional System," is not just a deviation from conventional knowledge; it is a call to arms for those who dare to attack the basic basis upon which the traditional concept of retirement is founded.

For generations, we've been conditioned to believe in the sanctity of accumulating a significant nest egg, a financial reserve to sustain us through the golden years. Yet, as we delve into the various layers of this age-old myth, we begin to learn that the story created around the nest egg is far from an infallible blueprint for riches. It's time to address the difficult truth that the old method of saving for retirement is, in essence, a myth – a well-intentioned but fundamentally flawed story that no longer corresponds with the realities of wealth building and enjoyment in the 21st century.

The thesis of this book develops as a revelation: the traditional approach to retirement, with its concentration on accumulating a fixed sum of money, fails to grasp the dynamic and interwoven nature of modern life. We will analyze how this misconception has left numerous individuals disillusioned, as they find themselves inadequately prepared for the uncertainties of the future. The stories are abundant — folks who carefully contributed to their nest eggs, only to have their financial ambitions dashed by economic downturns, unexpected health problems, or the altering landscape of retirement itself.

Consider the heartbreaking case of Jane, who dutifully tucked away monies in her nest egg throughout her career, only to realize that the inflationary erosion of her savings rendered her financial buffer woefully insufficient. Or the case of Mark, who followed the conventional wisdom of depending entirely on traditional investment vehicles, finding himself caught in the throes of market volatility and unable to recover the losses sustained during unforeseeable downturns.

As these stories develop, the realization becomes clear: the nest egg myth has left a path of failed hopes and unfulfilled promises. It's an antiquated narrative that fails to understand the varied nature of wealth — a concept that stretches beyond mere monetary value to embrace fulfillment, purpose, and the pursuit of a life well-lived.

This book, then, acts as a guide for individuals who dare to disrupt the current quo. It's an exploration of alternate paths to financial well-being and contentment, options that reach beyond the limits of the established system. As we navigate through the chapters, we will uncover unconventional strategies, emerging trends, and transformative perspectives that herald the dawn of a new era in personal finance – an era where building wealth and happiness is not restricted by outdated myths but shaped by innovation, adaptability, and a holistic understanding of true prosperity. It's time to start on a journey that surpasses the constraints of the nest egg myth and redefines the very essence of wealth generation and retirement in our ever-evolving society.

Read on and discover how to break free from the nest egg fallacy and enjoy the magnificent life you deserve!

Chapter 1

The Nest Egg Myth

Why Saving for Retirement is Not Enough

You have undoubtedly heard it many times before: prepare for retirement, invest in a 401(k) or IRA, diversify your portfolio, and live a comfortable life once you stop working. This is the common thinking that most people follow, and it is what the financial industry and the government want you to believe.

But what if I told you that this advice is not just outmoded, but also dangerous?

What if I told you that saving for retirement is not enough to safeguard your financial future and that relying on a nest egg could instead leave you poorer, unhappier, and more exposed to economic shocks and crises?

What if I told you that there is a better way to build wealth and happiness outside of the traditional system, a way that allows you more power, independence, and joy in your life?

In this chapter, I will reveal the flaws and pitfalls of the nest egg myth, and show you why you need to rethink your attitude to money and retirement. I will also introduce you to the four pillars of wealth, the power of passive income, and the wealth mindset, which are the essential concepts that will lead you throughout this book.

What is the Nest Egg Myth?

The nest egg fallacy is the assumption that saving and investing a substantial sum of money for retirement is the best and only method to achieve financial security and happiness. It is founded on the premise that you would work for a defined number of years, generate a regular income, and then retire at a predetermined age, usually 65 or older. It is also predicated on the premise that your nest fund will grow at a predictable rate, provide you with enough income to pay your expenses, and continue for the rest of your life.

The nest egg myth is so ubiquitous that it has become the default option for most people. It is what we are taught in school, what we see in the media, and what we hear from our friends and family. It is what the financial industry and the government promote and incentivize, through products like 401(k)s, IRAs, mutual funds, and Social Security.

The nest egg myth is particularly alluring because it looks simple and safe. All you have to do is save a portion of your salary, invest it in a diverse portfolio, and allow the magic of compound interest to do the work for you. You don't have to worry about anything else, just sit back and watch your money increase. And when you retire, you can enjoy the rewards of your efforts, travel the world, pursue your hobbies, and spend time with your loved ones.

Sounds good, right?

Well, not so fast.

The Flaws and Risks of the Nest Egg Myth

The problem with the nest egg myth is that it is built on a set of assumptions that are no longer valid, or never were in the first place. It is also built on a set of behaviors that are damaging to your financial health and happiness. Let's take a deeper look at some of the flaws and risks of the nest egg fallacy.

Flaw 1: It ignores the reality of the economy

The nest egg fallacy assumes that the economy is stable, predictable, and advantageous to saving and investors. It assumes that you will always have a job, that your income will always increase, that inflation will always be low, that interest rates will always be favorable, that taxes will always be reasonable, that the stock market will always go up, and that the government will always follow its commitments.

But as we have seen in the past several decades, and especially in the past few years, none of these assumptions are accurate. The economy is turbulent, uncertain, and hostile to savers and investors. We have witnessed:

- The dot-com bubble and bust of the late 1990s and early 2000s, wiped out trillions of dollars of wealth and millions of jobs.
- The worldwide financial crisis of 2008, which precipitated the worst recession since the Great Depression, and led millions of people to lose their homes, savings, and retirement accounts.
- The COVID-19 epidemic of 2020, which disturbed the entire world, shut down entire businesses and threw millions of people into poverty and unemployment.
- The extraordinary amounts of debt, deficit, and money creation by governments and central banks have undermined the value of money and generated huge inflation and currency devaluation. - The escalating levels of inequality, social unrest, and political instability, have heightened the possibility of civil war, revolution, and tyranny.

These are only some of the examples of the economic shocks and crises that have occurred in the recent past, and that could happen again in the near future. And these are not isolated events, but interconnected and systemic problems that are expected to grow over time.

The nest egg myth does not prepare you for these eventualities. In fact, it makes you more vulnerable to them. By saving and investing for retirement, you are exposing yourself to the whims and risks of the economy, the markets, and the government. You are putting your money in assets that can lose value, be taxed, confiscated, or stolen. You are reliant on sources of income that can be diminished, delayed, or eliminated. You are trusting institutions that can fail, cheat, or betray you.
You are essentially giving up control over your money and your life, and praying for the best.

But hope is not a strategy.

Flaw 2: It ignores the truth of human nature

The nest egg myth presumes that you are sensible, disciplined, and consistent in your financial decisions. It implies that you will always save a substantial amount of your money, that you will always invest sensibly and responsibly, that you will always keep to your plan, and that you will always resist the temptations and demands of consumerism, lifestyle inflation, and social comparison.

But as we all know, human nature is not so ideal. We are emotional, impulsive, and inconsistent in our financial judgments. We often:

- Fail to save enough, or at all, for numerous reasons, such as lack of money, lack of knowledge, lack of motivation, or lack of discipline.
- Fail to invest appropriately, or at all, for many reasons, such as lack of information, lack of confidence, lack of access, or lack of desire.
- Fail to follow our strategy, or change it constantly, for different reasons, such as lack of clarity, lack of commitment, lack of patience, or lack of flexibility.
- Fail to resist the temptations and demands of materialism, lifestyle inflation, and social comparison, for many reasons, such as lack of satisfaction, lack of purpose, loss of identity, or lack of self-esteem.

These are only some of the instances of the psychological and behavioral biases and barriers that impede us from saving and investing for retirement. And these are not odd or exceptional situations, but common and pervasive phenomena that influence most people.

The nest egg myth does not account for this reality. In fact, it exacerbates them. By saving and investing for retirement, you are setting yourself up for failure, frustration, and regret. You are putting your money into assets that are boring, complex, and remote. You are following a plan that is imprecise, strict, and long. You are pursuing a goal that is unknown, arbitrary, and postponed.

You are essentially trading your now for your future, and praying for the best.

But hope is not a strategy.

Flaw 3: It rejects the truth of life

The nest egg myth presumes that you are healthy, happy, and fulfilled in your profession and life. It implies that you like your job, that you have a decent work-life balance, that you have a supportive family and friends, that you have a significant purpose and passion, and that you have a positive outlook and attitude.

But as we all know, life is not so ideal. We often face:

- Health difficulties, such as chronic diseases, injuries, disabilities, or mental illnesses, impede our ability to work, earn, save, and invest.
- Happiness difficulties, such as stress, anxiety, sadness, or burnout, that impair our motivation, productivity, creativity, and performance.
- Fulfillment difficulties, such as boredom, dissatisfaction, resentment, or alienation, that diminish our interest, engagement, enjoyment, and fulfillment.
- Relationship troubles, such as disagreements, divorces, deaths, or estrangements, that bring us pain, grief, loneliness, or isolation.

- Purpose issues, such as perplexity, doubt, fear, or guilt, that inhibit our direction, vision, mission, or values.

These are only some of the examples of the personal and professional problems and difficulties that we meet in our work and life. And these are not unique or exceptional events, but common and unavoidable experiences that touch most people.

The nest egg myth does not respect these truths. In fact, it ignores them. By saving and investing for retirement, you are postponing your happiness and fulfillment, and praying for the best. You are putting your money into assets that are not aligned with your beliefs, aspirations, and dreams. You are following a strategy that is not appropriate to your personality, skills, and talents. You are pursuing a goal that is not aligned with your purpose, passion, and potential.

You are effectively living someone else's life, and hoping for the best.

But hope is not a strategy.

The Better Way to Build Wealth and Happiness Outside of the Traditional System

As you can see, the nest egg myth is not only incorrect but also risky. It is not the best and only approach to obtaining financial security and pleasure. It is not the way that I recommend you to follow.

Instead, I urge you to take an alternative strategy, a better method to build money and pleasure outside of the old system, a manner that provides you with more power, independence, and joy in your life.

This technique is based on three major principles:

- Principle 1: Don't save for retirement, save for financial independence.

- Principle 2: Don't invest in a nest egg, invest in passive income.

- **Principle 3:** Don't wait for retirement, live your greatest life now.

Certainly! Allow me to elaborate further on each of these principles.

Principle 1: Don't save for retirement, save for financial independence

The first concept is to change your thinking and goal from saving for retirement to saving for financial freedom.

What is the difference?

accumulating for retirement is accumulating and investing a sufficient sum of money that will provide you with adequate income to pay your costs when you stop working.

Saving for financial independence involves saving and investing enough money that will provide you with adequate income to cover your costs regardless of whether you work or not.

The difference is slight, but substantial.

Saving for retirement indicates that you are dependent on your employment for your income and that you will cease working at a specific age, usually 65 or older.
Saving for financial independence suggests that you are independent of your employment for your income and that you can choose to work or not at any age, based on your choices and circumstances.

Saving for retirement means that you are following a set and definite strategy and that you are hoping for the best.

Saving for financial independence implies that you are establishing your own adaptable strategy and that you are preparing for the worst.

Saving for retirement indicates that you are sacrificing your present for your future and that you are deferring your happiness and fulfillment.

Saving for financial independence indicates that you are optimizing your now and your future, and that you are boosting your pleasure and contentment.

Saving for retirement is predicated on the nest egg fallacy, which is erroneous and hazardous.

Saving for financial independence is founded on the four pillars of wealth, which are stable and reliable.

What are the four pillars of wealth?

They are income, assets, cash flow, and leverage.

Income is the money that you earn from your employment, such as salary, wages, commissions, bonuses, tips, etc.

Assets are the things that you possess that have worth, such as real estate, equities, bonds, gold, cryptocurrency, etc.

Cash flow is the money that you receive from your assets, such as rent, dividends, interest, royalties, etc.

Leverage is the use of other people's money, time, skills, or resources to boost your revenue, assets, or cash flow, such as loans, mortgages, partnerships, outsourcing, etc.

The four pillars of wealth are the foundation of your financial independence. They are the sources of your passive income, which is the key to your financial freedom.

What is passive income?

Passive income is the money that you earn without working, or with minimal work, such as cash flow from your assets, revenue from your web business, royalties from your book, etc.

Passive income is the opposite of active income, which is the money that you obtain from working, or with a lot of work, such as income from your employment, income from your freelance work, or income from your consulting business, etc.

Passive income is the power of your financial independence. It is the revenue that allows you to cover your expenses regardless of whether you work or not. It is the income that provides you with more power, freedom, and fulfillment in your life.

How do you acquire financial independence?

You obtain financial independence by raising your passive income until it exceeds your expenses.

This is the basic and straightforward formula of financial independence:

Passive Income > Expenses = Financial Independence

When your passive income is higher than your expenses, you are financially independent. You have enough money to live your desired lifestyle without working, or with minimal work. You have attained the ultimate goal of your financial path.

How do you enhance your passive income?

You enhance your passive income by applying the four pillars of wealth:

- You raise your income by working more, working smarter, working better, or working differently.
- You improve your assets by saving more, investing more, investing better, or investing differently.
- You enhance your cash flow by creating more, creating better, creating differently, or creating passively.
- You enhance your leverage by borrowing more, borrowing better, borrowing differently, or borrowing wisely.

These are the ideas and approaches that you will study and execute throughout this book. They will help you to grow your passive income, and ultimately, your financial independence.

But why should you invest for financial independence, instead of saving for retirement?

There are several benefits and advantages of saving for financial independence, compared to saving for retirement. Here are some of them:

- You can reach financial freedom sooner than retirement. Depending on your income, assets, cash flow, leverage, expenses, and lifestyle, you can attain financial independence in as little as a few years, or as long as a few decades. You don't have to wait till you are 65 or older to enjoy your financial freedom. You may do it at any age, whether you are in your 20s, 30s, 40s, 50s, or beyond.
- You can reach financial freedom with less money than retirement. Depending on your income, assets, cash flow, leverage, expenses, and lifestyle, you can attain financial

independence with as little as a few hundred thousand dollars, or as much as a few million dollars. You don't have to save and invest a significant amount of money that will give you adequate income to cover your costs after you quit working. You can save and invest enough money that will provide you with enough income to cover your expenses regardless of whether you work or not.

- You can reach financial independence with more stability than retirement. Depending on your income, assets, cash flow, debt, expenses, and lifestyle, you can reach financial independence with more diversification, protection, and resilience than retirement. You don't have to rely on a single source of income, such as your nest money, that can lose value, be taxed, confiscated, or stolen. You can rely on numerous sources of income, such as your passive income, that can increase, compound, and sustain you.
- You can reach financial freedom with more enjoyment than retirement. Depending on your income, assets, cash flow, leverage, spending, and lifestyle, you can attain

financial independence with more satisfaction, purpose, and fulfillment than retirement. You don't have to sacrifice your present for your future and postpone your happiness and fulfillment. You may optimize your current and your future, and boost your happiness and contentment.

These are only some of the benefits and advantages of investing for financial independence, compared to saving for retirement. There are many more that you will find and experience as you embark on your financial independence journey.

But saving for financial independence is not enough. You also need to invest in passive income, which is the second premise of the better approach to generating wealth and pleasure outside of the existing system.

Principle 2: Don't invest in a nest egg, invest in passive income

- You can produce passive income with more flexibility than a nest egg. Depending on your income, assets, cash flow, leverage, expenses, and lifestyle, you can produce passive income from a variety of sources, such as real estate, enterprises, royalties, etc. You don't have to place your money in things that are boring, complex, and remote, such as stocks, bonds, mutual funds, etc. You can put your money in assets that are interesting, straightforward, and close, such as properties, products, services, etc.

- You can earn passive income with more control than a nest fund. Depending on your income, assets, cash flow, leverage, expenses, and lifestyle, you can produce passive income by building, enhancing, renting, selling, or licensing your assets, either by yourself or with others. You don't have to depend on the success of the economy, the markets, or the government, which are unpredictable and unreliable. You may count on your abilities, expertise, and inventiveness, which are predictable and reliable.

- You can earn passive income with more satisfaction than a nest fund. Depending on your income, assets, cash flow, leverage, expenses, and lifestyle, you can earn passive income that is aligned with your beliefs, aspirations, and desires. You don't have to sacrifice your present for your future and postpone your happiness and fulfillment. You may optimize your current and your future, and boost your happiness and contentment.

These are only some of the perks and advantages of investing in passive income, compared to investing in a nest fund. There are many more things you will discover and experience as you embark on your passive income adventure.

However, investing in passive income is not enough. You also need to live your best life now, which is the third principle of the better approach to generating wealth and happiness outside of the existing system.

Principle 3: Don't wait for retirement, live your best life now

The third point is to transform your mindset and action from waiting for retirement to living your best life now.

What is the difference?

Waiting for retirement implies deferring your happiness and fulfillment till you quit working, and hoping for the best.

Living your best life now involves enjoying your happiness and fulfillment while you are working, and preparing for the worst.

The difference is slight, but substantial.

Waiting for retirement means that you are not happy and pleased with your work and life and that you are looking forward to the day when you can quit your job and pursue what you love.

Living your best life now suggests that you are happy and fulfilled with your work and life and that you are not waiting for the day when you can quit your job and do what you love, but rather, you are doing what you love and quitting your job when you want.

Waiting for retirement implies that you are following someone else's plan and that you are hoping for the best.

Living your best life now implies that you are developing your plan and that you are prepared for the worst.

Waiting until retirement suggests that you are sacrificing your now for your future and that you are postponing your happiness and fulfillment.

Living your best life now indicates that you are optimizing your present and your future and that you are boosting your pleasure and fulfillment.

Waiting for retirement is based on the nest egg myth, which is flawed and risky.

Living your best life now is based on a wealthy lifestyle, which is solid and reliable.

What is the wealthy lifestyle?

The wealth lifestyle is the way of living that allows you to enjoy your money and your life, without compromising your financial independence or your happiness and fulfillment.

The wealth lifestyle is the opposite of the poverty lifestyle, which is the manner of living that hinders you from enjoying your money and your life, and undermines your financial freedom and your happiness and fulfillment.

The wealthy lifestyle is the secret to your financial happiness. It is the lifestyle that allows you to live your ideal lifestyle without working, or with minimum employment. It is the lifestyle that gives you more power, independence, and fulfillment in your life.

How can you acquire a wealthy lifestyle?

You reach the wealth lifestyle by applying the four pillars of wealth:

- You raise your income by working more, working smarter, working better, or working differently.
- You improve your assets by saving more, investing more, investing better, or investing differently.
- You enhance your cash flow by creating more, creating better, creating differently, or creating passively.
- You enhance your leverage by borrowing more, borrowing better, borrowing differently, or borrowing wisely.

These are the ideas and approaches that you will study and execute throughout this book. They will help you to establish your wealthy lifestyle, and eventually, your financial happiness.

But why should you live your greatest life now, instead of waiting until retirement?

There are many benefits and advantages of enjoying your best life now, compared to waiting for retirement. Here are some of them:

- You can live your greatest life today sooner than retirement. Depending on your income, assets, cash flow, leverage, expenses, and lifestyle, you can live your best life now in as little as a few months, or as long as a few years. You don't have to wait till you stop working to enjoy your money and your life. You can enjoy your money and your life while you are working, or with minimum work.

- You can live your greatest life now with less money than retirement. Depending on your income, assets, cash flow, leverage, spending, and lifestyle, you can live your greatest life now with as little as a few thousand dollars, or as much as a few hundred thousand dollars. You don't have to save and invest a significant amount of money that will give you adequate income to cover your costs after you quit working. You can save and invest enough money that will provide you with enough income to cover your expenses regardless of whether you work or not.

- You can live your best life today with more security than retirement. Depending on your income, assets, cash flow, leverage, expenses, and lifestyle, you can live your greatest life today with more diversification, safety, and resilience than retirement. You don't have to rely on a single source of income, such as your nest money, that can lose value, be taxed, confiscated, or stolen. You can rely on numerous sources of income, such as your passive income, that can increase, compound, and sustain you.
- You can live your best life now with more satisfaction than retirement. Depending on your income, assets, cash flow, leverage, spending, and lifestyle, you can live your best life today with greater satisfaction, meaning, and fulfillment than retirement. You don't have to sacrifice your present for your future and postpone your happiness and fulfillment. You may optimize your current and your future, and boost your happiness and contentment.

These are only some of the perks and advantages of enjoying your greatest life now, as opposed to waiting for retirement. There are many more things you will discover and experience as you embark on your rich lifestyle adventure.

Conclusion

In this chapter, I have highlighted the weaknesses and perils of the nest egg myth and demonstrated why you need to rethink your attitude toward money and retirement. I have also presented you with the superior approach to developing money and happiness outside of the traditional system, which is based on three basic principles:

- Don't save for retirement, save for financial independence.
- Don't invest in a nest egg, invest in passive income.
- Don't wait for retirement, live your best life now.

These ideas will guide you throughout this book, and allow you to attain your financial independence, your passive income, and your rich lifestyle.

But before we dig into the intricacies of how to implement these concepts, we need to understand how we got here in the first place. We need to understand the history and evolution of the global system, and how it has impacted our views and habits regarding money and retirement.

That is the theme of the following chapter, where I will explain how we got here, and what are the incorrect allocations that we need to overcome.

I hope you enjoyed this chapter, and that you are interested to discover more.

Chapter 2

The Wealth Evolution in the Global System

Wealth is one of the most essential notions in human history. It is the measure of the worth of the resources, assets, and income that we possess or control. It is also the source of our power, influence, and well-being. But what is wealth, and how has it evolved over time?

In this chapter, we will analyze how wealth has changed from the Stone Age to the present day, and how diverse elements such as natural resources, human capital, technology, and institutions have influenced wealth generation and distribution. We will also study how wealth impacts our happiness, health, and social ties, and how it shapes our views and behavior regarding money and retirement.

What is Wealth?

Wealth can be defined as the store of economic value that can be used to generate income or consumption. Wealth can be classified into two basic categories: tangible and intangible.

- Tangible wealth is the physical and financial assets that can be seen and touched, such as land, buildings, machinery, equipment, cattle, crops, minerals, metals, fossil fuels, and money.
- Intangible wealth is the non-physical and non-financial assets that cannot be seen or touched, yet have economic worth, such as human capital, social capital, natural capital, intellectual capital, and institutional capital.

Human capital is the value of the skills, knowledge, health, and capacities of individuals. Social capital is the value of trust, cooperation, and networks among individuals. Natural capital is the worth of the ecosystems, biodiversity, and environmental services that support life on Earth. Intellectual capital is the value of the ideas, innovations, and inventions that create new products, services, and processes. Institutional capital is the value of the rules, conventions, and structures that govern the conduct and interactions of people and groups.

Wealth can be quantified at several levels, such as person, home, community, country, region, or planet. Wealth can also be quantified in many ways, such as net worth, income, consumption, or well-being. Different metrics of wealth can capture different characteristics of wealth, but they can also have different limitations and biases.

For example, net worth is the difference between the entire value of the assets and the total value of the liabilities that a person or a group owns or owes. Net worth can represent the financial situation and security of a person or a group, but it can also exclude other forms of intangible wealth, such as human capital or social capital, that are not easily measured or accounted for.

Income is the flow of money or goods that a person or a group receives or earns from numerous sources, such as wages, salaries, profits, rents, dividends, interest, transfers, or gifts. Income can reflect the earning potential and purchasing power of an individual or a group, but it can also fluctuate over time and depend on different factors, such as market circumstances, business cycles, taxes, subsidies, or legislation.

Consumption is the quantity of money or things that a person or a group spends or utilizes for various purposes, such as food, clothes, housing, education, health, entertainment, or travel. Consumption can represent the living standards and contentment of a person or a group, but it can also reflect the preferences and choices of a person or a group, which can differ between cultures, contexts, and situations.

Well-being encompasses the condition of having joy, robust health, and flourishing prosperity.

Well-being can reflect the quality of life and happiness of a person or a community, but it can also be subjective and multifaceted, involving different components, such as physical, mental, emotional, social, spiritual, and environmental dimensions.

How has Wealth Evolved over Time?

Wealth has evolved over time, from the Stone Age to the current day, in terms of its quantity, quality, diversity, and distribution. We can divide the evolution of wealth into four key stages: the hunter-gatherer stage, the agricultural stage, the industrial stage, and the post-industrial period.

The Hunter-Gatherer Stage

The hunter-gatherer era is the earliest and longest stage of human history, lasting from roughly 2.5 million years ago to about 10,000 years ago. In this era, humans lived in small and nomadic groups, dependent on hunting, fishing, and gathering wild plants and animals for their sustenance. They had no permanent settlements, no domesticated animals, no cultivated crops, no written language, no money, and no formal institutions. Their prosperity was mostly based on natural capital, such as land, water, forests, wildlife, and climate. Their wealth was also restricted by the availability and fluctuation of natural resources, the carrying capacity of the ecosystem, and the competition and collaboration with other tribes.

The hunter-gatherer period was marked by low levels of prosperity, but also by high levels of egalitarianism and well-being. According to some estimates, the average income of a hunter-gatherer was roughly $1.10 per day (in 1990 international dollars), which is below the poverty line of $1.90 per day (in 2011 international dollars) set by the World Bank. However, the hunter-gatherers also had low levels of consumption, low levels of population, low levels of sickness, low levels of violence, and high levels of leisure, independence, and happiness. According to some studies, the hunter-gatherers worked only around 15 to 20 hours per week, had more than 100 days of rest per year, and enjoyed more than 10 hours of sleep per day. They also had strong social relationships, egalitarian standards, and democratic decision-making inside their groups.

The Agricultural Stage

The agricultural stage is the second stage of human history, lasting from around 10,000 years ago until roughly 250 years ago. In this stage, humans established agriculture, the domestication of plants and animals, and the cultivation of crops and livestock. They also established sedentary and hierarchical societies, with permanent settlements, cities, governments, empires, civilizations, and religions. They also created writing, mathematics, physics, art, literature, and philosophy. They also developed money, trade, markets, and institutions. Their wealth was mostly based on physical capital, such as land, buildings, machinery, equipment, animals, crops, minerals, metals, and money. Their riches were also improved by the increase and improvement of natural resources, human capital, technology, and institutions.

The agricultural period was marked by great levels of prosperity, but also by high levels of inequality and poor levels of well-being. According to some estimates, the average salary of an agriculturalist was roughly $3.10 per day (in 1990 international dollars), which is over the poverty line of $1.90 per day (in 2011 international dollars) set by the World Bank. However, the agriculturalists also had high levels of consumption, high levels of population, high levels of sickness, high levels of violence, and poor levels of leisure, independence, and happiness. According to several researches, the agriculturalists worked between 40 to 60 hours per week, had less than 50 days of rest per year, and suffered from more than 5 hours of sleep deprivation each day. They also had weak social bonds, unequal norms, and authoritarian decision-making inside their cultures.

The Industrial Stage

The industrial period is the third stage of human history, extending from about 250 years ago to around 50 years ago. In this stage, mankind experienced the Industrial Revolution, the rapid and broad restructuring of the economy, society, and culture by the application of science, technology, and invention to production, transportation, communication, and consumption. They also underwent the demographic transition, the move from high birth rates and high death rates to low birth rates and low death rates, resulting in population expansion, urbanization, and aging. They also underwent the political transition, the shift from monarchy, aristocracy, and colonialism to democracy, republicanism, and nationalism, resulting in revolutions, wars, and movements. They also experienced the social transition, the shift from tradition, religion, and community to modernity, secularism, and individualism, resulting in reforms, changes, and problems. Their fortune was mostly built on financial capital, such as money, stocks, bonds, and derivatives. Their riches were also increased by the rise and development of natural resources, human capital, technology, and institutions.

The industrial period was marked by very high levels of prosperity, but also by very high levels of inequality and very low levels of well-being. According to some estimates, the average income of an industrialist was over $33.10 per day (in 1990 international dollars), which is significantly above the poverty line of $1.90 per day (in 2011 international dollars) specified by the World Bank. However, the industrialists also had very high levels of consumption, very high levels of population, very high levels of sickness, very high levels of violence, and very low levels of leisure, freedom, and happiness. According to several researches, the industrialists worked roughly 60 to 80 hours per week, had less than 10 days of rest per year, and suffered from more than 7 hours of sleep deprivation each day. They also had poor social bonds, unequal rules, and dishonest decision-making within their cultures.

The Post-Industrial Stage

The post-industrial period is the current and fourth stage of human history, stretching from around 50 years ago to the present day. In this stage, mankind is experiencing the Information Revolution, the rapid and broad transformation of the economy, society, and culture by the application of science, technology, and innovation to information, knowledge, communication, and education. They are also experiencing the ecological transition, the move from exploiting, deteriorating, and polluting the environment to preserving, repairing, and safeguarding the environment, resulting in crises, disputes, and solutions. They are also witnessing the cultural transition, the shift from homogeneity, conformity, and stability to diversity, plurality, and change, resulting in globalization, migration, and integration. They are also experiencing the personal transition, the move from materialism, rationality, and individualism to spirituality, intuition, and collectivism, leading to transformation, awakening, and enlightenment. Their wealth is mostly built on intangible capital, such as human capital, social capital, natural capital, intellectual capital, and institutional capital. Their wealth is also determined by the fall and renewal of natural resources, human capital, technology, and institutions.

The post-industrial stage is marked by very high levels of wealth, but also by very high levels of inequality and very low levels of well-being. According to some estimates, the average income of a post-industrialist is about $101.10 per day (in 1990 international dollars), which is well over the poverty level of $1.90 per day (in 2011 international dollars) specified by the World Bank. However, the post-industrialists also have extremely high levels of consumption, very high levels of population, very high levels of sickness, very high levels of violence, and very low levels of leisure, freedom, and happiness. According to several researchers, post-industrialists work roughly 80 to 100 hours per week, have less than 5 days of rest per year, and suffer from more than 9 hours of sleep deprivation each day. They also have poor social bonds, unequal rules, and dishonest decision-making within their cultures.

How Does Wealth Affect Our Happiness, Health, and Social Relations?

Wealth influences our enjoyment, health, and social relations in numerous ways, both positive and negative. On the one hand, wealth can provide us with the means and chances to satisfy our basic requirements, such as food, shelter, clothing, education, and health care. Wealth can also empower us to pursue our higher wants, such as self-actualization, creativity, and spirituality. Wealth can also boost our sense of security, independence, and autonomy. Wealth can also boost our social position, respect, and recognition. Wealth can also facilitate our social relationships, cooperation, and contribution. Wealth can also enrich our experiences, diversity, and learning.

On the other hand, riches may also cause or intensify our issues and challenges, such as greed, envy, pride, and arrogance. Wealth can also trigger or intensify our stress, worry, and despair. Wealth can also erode or distort our values, morality, and ethics. Wealth can also impair or damage our enjoyment, health, and social relations. Wealth can also cause or intensify disputes, bloodshed, and injustice. Wealth can sometimes limit or constrict our choices, options, and alternatives. Wealth can also hinder or inhibit our growth, development, and fulfillment.

The relationship between wealth and happiness, health, and social relations is complicated and dynamic, dependent on several aspects, such as the amount, kind, source, distribution, and use of wealth, as well as the background, culture, and position of the people and groups involved. There is no simple or universal formula or rule that can determine or predict the consequences of wealth on human well-being. However, there are certain broad concepts and recommendations that can help us understand and optimize the influence of wealth on our happiness, health, and social ties, such as:

- The law of diminishing returns: The more wealth we have, the less extra wealth boosts our pleasure, health, and social interactions. Beyond a certain point, more wealth may even reduce our well-being, since the costs and hazards of wealth outweigh the pleasures and rewards of wealth.

- The paradox of choice: The more riches we have, the more choices and options we have. However, too many choices and possibilities can also overwhelm and confuse us, leaving us less content and more regretful about our selections.

- The hedonic treadmill: The more riches we have, the more we adapt and adjust to our new level of prosperity, making us less appreciative and more demanding of our wealth. We also tend to compare ourselves with others who have more wealth, making us less pleased and more jealous of our fortune.

- The social comparison: The more riches we have, the more we compare ourselves with others who have less wealth, making us more proud and arrogant of our wealth. We also tend to remove ourselves from others who have less riches, making us less empathic and caring about our fortune.

- Relative deprivation: The more riches we have, the more we feel deprived and unsatisfied of our prosperity if we consider that others have more wealth or that we deserve more wealth. We also tend to dislike and blame others who have more riches, making us more furious and resentful of our prosperity.

- The altruistic effect: The more wealth we have, the more we can give and contribute our wealth to others who have less wealth, making us more giving and kind with our fortune. We also tend to feel better and healthier when we utilize our riches for prosocial goals, such as assisting, supporting, and donating to others.

How does Wealth Shape our Beliefs and Behavior about Money and Retirement?

Wealth impacts our attitudes and behavior regarding money and retirement in numerous ways, both conscious and unconscious. Our thoughts and behavior concerning money and retirement are influenced by our personal, social, and cultural elements, such as our personality, upbringing, education, experience, values, goals, motives, emotions, attitudes, expectations, norms, roles, and identities. Our thoughts and behavior about money and retirement are also affected by our economic, political, and environmental aspects, such as our income, wealth, occupation, status, power, influence, security, stability, opportunity, risk, uncertainty, change, and challenge.

Our thoughts and behavior about money and retirement can be grouped into four broad groups, based on the degree of alignment or misalignment between our wealth and our well-being. These types are:

- The Satisfied: Those who have enough riches and enough well-being, and are pleased and content with their money and retirement. They have a balanced and healthy relationship with money and retirement, based on gratitude, satisfaction, and fulfillment. They use their money and retirement wisely and responsibly, for their own and others' benefit. They have a good and realistic attitude toward money and retirement, based on optimism, confidence, and resilience.

- The Struggling: Those who have enough wealth but not enough well-being, who are unhappy and unsatisfied with their money and retirement. They have an unstable and toxic relationship with money and retirement, based on greed, envy, and pride. They utilize their money and retirement unwisely and carelessly, for their own and others' detriment. They have a negative and erroneous attitude toward money and retirement, based on pessimism, insecurity, and fragility.

- The Aspiring: Those who have not enough riches but enough well-being, and are hopeful and motivated with their money and retirement. They have a demanding and satisfying relationship with money and retirement, based on ambition, goal, and achievement. They use their money and retirement efficiently and successfully, for their own and others' improvement. They have a good and realistic attitude toward money and retirement, based on optimism, confidence, and resilience.

- The Suffering: Those who have not enough riches and not enough well-being, and are despairing and desperate with their money and retirement. They have a stressful and painful relationship with money and retirement, centered on dread, anxiety, and depression. They use their money and retirement improperly and ineffectively, for their own and others' damage. They have a negative and erroneous attitude toward money and retirement, based on pessimism, insecurity, and fragility.

These categories are not fixed or permanent but can change over time and between contexts, depending on many elements and conditions. However, these types can also become self-reinforcing and self-perpetuating, generating a vicious or virtuous cycle of riches and well-being. Therefore, it is crucial to be aware and observant of our ideas and behavior regarding money and retirement and to seek and embrace the best practices and habits that can boost our wealth and well-being.

Chapter 3

The Four Pillars of Wealth

Many individuals assume that the only way to develop wealth is to save money in a retirement account, such as a 401(k) or an IRA, and hope that it will grow enough to provide them with a comfortable income in their golden years. This is what we call the **nest egg myth**. The nest egg fallacy is founded on the belief that you can rely on the stock market, the government, and your job to take care of your financial future. However, this assumption is dangerous and typically leads to disappointment, frustration, and stress.

The nest egg myth is not the only way to build wealth. In reality, it is not even the best way. There is a better way, a way that provides you more power, more freedom, and more enjoyment. This technique is built on the four pillars of wealth: income, assets, cash flow, and leverage. These four pillars are the core of a successful wealth-building strategy that

can help you reach your financial objectives and live
the life you want.

Income

Income is the money that you earn from your labor, your business, or your investments. Income is vital since it allows you to cover your living needs, pay off your obligations, and invest in your future. However, money alone is not enough to build wealth. Income is merely a means to an aim, not an end in itself. Income is also restricted by your time, your abilities, and your market value. You can only work so many hours, you can only charge so much for your services, and you can only earn so much from your assets. Therefore, income is not the ultimate measure of wealth, but rather a vehicle to obtain the other pillars of prosperity.

Assets

Assets are the things that you possess that have worth and can generate revenue for you. Assets include items like real estate, businesses, equities, bonds, commodities, cryptocurrency, art, collectibles, and intellectual property. Assets are crucial since they are the source of your wealth. Assets can appreciate in value over time, provide you with passive income, and protect you against inflation and economic downturns. However, not all assets are created equal. Some assets are more productive, more liquid, and more tax-efficient than others. Therefore, you need to be selective and strategic about the assets that you purchase and how you manage them.

Cash Flow

Cash flow is the gap between the income that you receive and the expenses that you pay. Cash flow is crucial since it impacts your financial health and your ability to develop your wealth. Cash flow can be positive or negative. Positive cash flow suggests that you have more money coming in than going out. Negative cash flow suggests that you have more money going out than coming in. Positive cash flow is critical for developing wealth because it allows you to save more, invest more, and borrow more. Negative cash flow is negative for developing wealth because it forces you to borrow more, spend less, and sell your assets. Therefore, you need to monitor and optimize your cash flow by increasing your income, minimizing your expenses, and controlling your debts.

Leverage

Leverage is the utilization of other people's resources to amplify your results. Leverage can be financial, such as utilizing debt to buy more assets, or non-financial, such as exploiting other people's time, skills, knowledge, network, or reputation to achieve your aims. Leverage is vital because it helps you to do more with less, to double your income, assets, and cash flow, and to accelerate your wealth growth. However, leverage also comes with hazards, such as interest, fees, obligations, and liabilities. Therefore, you need to use leverage intelligently and responsibly, by knowing the costs and advantages, the risks and rewards, and the possibilities and dangers.

Conclusion

The four pillars of wealth: income, assets, cash flow, and leverage, are the main aspects of a successful wealth-building approach. By mastering these four pillars, you may construct a solid financial foundation, produce several streams of income, grow your net worth, and achieve financial freedom and happiness. The nest egg myth is not the only way to acquire wealth, and it is not even the greatest one. There is a better way, a way that is founded on the four pillars of riches. This way is the way of the wealthy, and it can be your way too.

Chapter 4

The Power of Passive Income

How to Create Multiple Streams of Income Without Working More

One of the major obstacles that people experience while trying to generate wealth is the lack of time. Time is a scarce and finite resource that we all have to manage and prioritize. Time is also the key element that restricts our financial potential. No matter how hard we work, how much we charge, or how many hours we put in, we can only earn so much from our active income. Active income is the revenue that we make from our work, our business, or our assets that need our direct engagement and effort. Active income is based on our time, and time is not scalable.

However, there is another sort of income that is not restricted by time, that is scalable, and that may help us attain our financial goals faster and easier. This form of revenue is termed passive income. Passive income is the revenue that we get from our assets, our business, or our investments that do not require our direct involvement and work. Passive income is independent of our time, yet time is leverageable.

Passive income is the key to growing wealth and pleasure because it allows us to develop various streams of income without working more. Passive income allows us greater freedom, more flexibility, and more security. Passive income enables us to live the lifestyle we want, to pursue our passions and interests, and to enjoy our lives more. Passive income is the power of wealth, and it can be your power too.

What is Passive Income?

Passive income is the income that you make without actively working for it. Passive income is the reverse of active income, which is the income that you earn by exchanging your time and energy for money. Passive income is also different from portfolio income, which is the income that you generate from your investments, such as dividends, interest, or capital gains. Portfolio income can be passive or active, depending on how much you are involved in managing your investments.

Passive income is not free money, nor is it easy money. Passive income takes an initial input of time, money, or both, to construct or purchase an asset that can generate income for you. Passive income also requires some maintenance and monitoring, to verify that your asset is working well and generating the appropriate outcomes. Passive income is not a get-rich-quick program, nor is it a lazy way to create money. Passive income is a smart and deliberate approach to creating money, by using your resources and producing value for others.

Why is Passive Income Important?

Passive income is significant for many reasons, but here are some of the key benefits of passive income:

- Passive income boosts your income potential. Passive income allows you to earn more money without working more hours, by creating various streams of income that can run on autopilot. Passive income can augment your active income, or perhaps replace it totally, depending on your goals and preferences. Passive income can help you attain financial independence, which is the status of having enough income to pay for your living needs without having to work.

- Passive income diversifies your revenue streams. Passive income decreases your reliance on a single source of income, such as your employment, your business, or your investments. Passive income protects you from the risks and uncertainties of the economy, the market, and the industry. Passive income offers you a safety net, a backup plan, and a buffer, in case something goes wrong with your primary income source. Passive income gives you peace of mind, knowing that you have various options and opportunities to produce money.

- Passive revenue frees up your time. Passive income allows you to work less, or not at all, by creating cash for you without your ongoing engagement and effort. Passive income allows you more time to do the things that you love, such as spending time with your family and friends, exploring the world, acquiring new skills, or pursuing your hobbies and passions. Passive income allows you greater control over your schedule, your pace, and your priorities. Passive income allows you more flexibility, more balance, and more enjoyment.

How to Create Passive Income?

Passive money can be made in many ways, but here are some of the more common and popular techniques for creating passive income:

- Real estate. Real estate is one of the most common and effective ways to produce passive income, by owning and renting out properties, such as houses, flats, offices, or land. Real estate can give you a reliable and constant income from rent, as well as appreciation and tax benefits from ownership. Real estate can also be leveraged, by utilizing loans to buy new properties, or by leveraging other people's money to support your acquisitions. Real estate needs a large amount of capital, experience, and management, but it may also offer a high return on investment and a long-term cash flow.

- Business. firm is another popular and effective approach to produce passive income, by founding or acquiring a firm that can operate without your direct involvement and work. Businesses can give you income

from sales, earnings, or royalties, as well as equity and tax benefits from ownership. firm can also be leveraged, by leveraging systems, processes, and technology to automate your operations, or by employing other
people's time, skills, and network to manage your firm. Business demands a lot of imagination, invention, and leadership, but it can also provide a lot of value, impact, and legacy.

- Online. Online is one of the most accessible and scalable ways to make passive income, by building or acquiring an online asset that can generate revenue for you on the internet. Online assets include items like websites, blogs, podcasts, movies, courses, ebooks, software, apps, or online platforms. Online assets can provide you with income via advertising, subscriptions, memberships, affiliates, or products, as well as exposure and influence from the online public. Online assets can also be used, by employing tools, platforms, and methods to optimize your traffic, conversions, and revenue. Online assets demand a lot of content, promotion, and interaction, but they may also reach a worldwide market, a niche audience, and a committed community.

Conclusion

Passive income is the income that you make without actively working for it. Passive income is the key to increasing wealth and pleasure because it allows you to develop several streams of income without working more. Passive income allows you greater freedom, more flexibility, and more security. Passive income enables you to live the lifestyle you want, to pursue your passions and interests, and to enjoy your life more. Passive income is the power of wealth, and it can be your power too.

Chapter 5

The Wealth Mindset

How to Overcome Fear, Scarcity, and Limiting Beliefs

One of the main hurdles that people confront while trying to earn wealth is their own thinking. Mindset is the set of beliefs, attitudes, and assumptions that shape our experience of reality and influence our behavior. Mindset is the prism through which we see the world and ourselves. Mindset is the filter that determines what we think, feel, and do.

Mindset is also the key to building wealth and pleasure because it dictates how we approach our financial goals and difficulties. Mindset may either empower us or limit us, inspire us or discourage us, motivate us, or hold us back. Mindset can either help us or harm us, depending on whether we have a wealth mindset or a poverty attitude.

A wealth mindset is the mindset of the wealthy, the successful, and the joyful. A rich mindset is focused on plenty, confidence, and possibilities. A wealth mindset is a mindset that permits us to produce and attract wealth and happiness in our lives.

A poverty mindset is the mindset of the poor, the suffering, and the unhappy. A poor mindset is founded on fear, scarcity, and limitation. A poverty mindset is the thinking that inhibits us from creating and attracting riches and pleasure in our lives.

In this chapter, we will discuss the contrasts between the wealth mindset and the poverty mindset, and how to overcome the fear, scarcity, and limiting ideas that keep us bound in the poverty mindset. We will also learn how to build a wealth mindset, and how to use it to attain our financial objectives and live our dream life.

The Wealth Mindset vs. The Poverty Mindset

The riches mindset and the poverty mindset are two opposed and contrasting ways of thinking and feeling about money, wealth, and happiness. They are not defined by how much money we have, but by how we connect to money and wealth. They are neither fixed nor permanent, but flexible and adaptable. They are neither inherited nor predetermined but learned and chosen.

Here are some of the fundamental distinctions between the wealth mindset and the poverty mindset:

- The wealth mindset believes that money is abundant, that there is enough for everyone, and that money can be created and increased. The poverty mindset believes that money is rare, that there is not enough for everyone, and that money can only be split and lost.
- The wealth mindset sees money as a tool, a resource, and a means to an end. The poverty

mindset sees money as a goal, a necessity, and an end in itself.

- The wealth mindset values money for what it can do, for the opportunities, experiences, and impact that it can give. The poverty mindset appreciates money for what it is, for the stability, status, and identity that it may bring.
- The wealth mindset uses money to generate value, solve issues, and help others. The poverty mindset uses money to consume, hoard, and protect oneself.
- The wealth mindset is grateful for what it has and generous with what it can give. The poor mindset is bitter about what it lacks and stingy with what it can share.
- The wealth mindset is cheerful, enthusiastic, and hopeful. The poor mindset is pessimistic, negative, and scared.
- The wealth mindset is proactive, action-oriented, and solution-focused. The poverty mindset is reactive, passive, and problem-focused.
- The wealth mindset is growth-oriented, learning-oriented, and improvement-oriented.

The poor mindset is fixed-oriented, comfort-oriented, and maintenance-oriented.

- The wealth mindset is open-minded, inquiring, and adaptable. The impoverished mindset is closed-minded, dogmatic, and unyielding.
- The wealth mindset is confident, fearless, and resilient. The impoverished mindset is insecure, scared, and vulnerable.

These are only some of the examples of how the prosperity mindset and the poverty mindset differ in their beliefs and attitudes toward money, wealth, and happiness. As you can see, the wealth mindset is more beneficial to generating wealth and happiness, while the poverty mindset is more destructive to building wealth and happiness. Therefore, if we want to attain our financial goals and live our ideal life, we need to adopt the wealthy attitude and avoid the poverty mindset.

The nest egg myth

How to Overcome Fear, Scarcity, and Limiting Beliefs

One of the main reasons why we have the poverty mindset is because we have fear, scarcity, and limiting ideas that hold us back from producing and attracting prosperity and pleasure in our lives. Fear, scarcity, and limiting ideas are the adversaries of the wealth mindset, and they need to be overcome if we want to achieve and grow.

Fear is the emotion that we feel when we sense a threat or a risk, real or imagined, that can injure us or hinder us from attaining our goals. Fear can be useful and helpful when it signals us to a genuine risk or difficulty that we need to face or avoid. Fear may sometimes be damaging and debilitating when it exaggerates or creates a false or unreasonable risk or difficulty that we need to conquer or ignore.

Scarcity is the state or feeling of having less than enough or lacking something that we need or want. Scarcity might be actual or perceived, objective or subjective, relative or absolute. Scarcity can be created by external reasons, such as limited resources, competition, or demand, or by internal factors, such as low self-esteem, high expectations, or poor habits. Scarcity can also be a mindset, a style of thinking and feeling that focuses on what we don't have, rather than on what we do have.

Limiting beliefs are the thoughts and assumptions that we have about ourselves, others, and the world, that limit our potential and possibilities. Limiting beliefs are generally founded on fear, scarcity, or negative experiences, that affect our vision of reality and influence our behavior. Limiting beliefs are typically subconscious, concealed, or ingrained, that we are not aware of or that we accept as true without questioning or challenging.

Fear, scarcity, and limiting beliefs are the key things that keep us in the poverty mindset and prevent us from producing and attracting prosperity and pleasure in our lives. They make us feel uneasy, incompetent, and unworthy. They make us doubt ourselves, our ability, and our possibilities. They make us avoid risks, challenges, and changes. They make us settle for less, sacrifice our ideals, and sabotage our progress.

Therefore, if we want to overcome the poverty mindset and embrace the wealth mindset, we need to overcome fear, scarcity, and limiting ideas. Here are a variety of approaches to accomplish this:

- Identify your fear, scarcity, and limiting beliefs. The first step to overcoming fear, scarcity, and limiting ideas is to recognize and admit them. You need to be honest and conscious of what you are frightened of, what you are lacking, and what you believe is holding you back from producing and attracting prosperity and pleasure in your life. You can utilize methods such as writing, meditation, coaching, or therapy, to help you uncover and understand your fear, scarcity, and limiting beliefs.
- Challenge your fear, scarcity, and limiting beliefs. The second stage to overcome fear, scarcity, and limiting ideas is to examine and dispute them. You need to be rational and logical and use data and facts, to prove that your fear, scarcity, and restricting ideas are not true, not legitimate, or not useful. You can use strategies like affirmations,

visualization, reframing, or cognitive behavioral therapy, to help you challenge and modify your fear, scarcity, and limiting beliefs.

- Replace your fear, scarcity, and limiting beliefs. The third stage to overcoming fear, scarcity, and limiting beliefs is to replace them with courage, abundance, and empowering beliefs. You need to be positive and optimistic and use emotions and actions, to establish and reinforce new ideas that support your prosperity and happiness goals. You can utilize strategies such as appreciation, giving, goal-setting, or action-taking, to help you replace and adopt new beliefs that match with the wealth mindset.

By following these methods, you can overcome fear, scarcity, and limiting ideas, and free yourself from the poverty mindset. You may also cultivate the wealth mindset, and use it to attain your financial goals and live your dream life.

How to Cultivate the Wealth Mindset

The wealth mindset is not something that you are born with, that you can buy, or that you can receive from someone else. The wealth mindset is something that you can build, cultivate, and grow, by yourself, for yourself, and with yourself. The wealth mindset is a talent, a habit, and a decision, that you can learn, practice, and make, every day, in every scenario, and in every part of your life.

Here are some of the strategies to create a wealth mindset:

- Educate yourself. The wealth mindset is founded on knowledge, information, and wisdom, that can help you comprehend and master money, wealth, and happiness. You need to educate yourself on the ideas, strategies, and techniques that can help you produce and attract prosperity and happiness in your life. You can use sources such as books, podcasts, classes, mentors, or experts, to help you learn and increase your financial literacy and intelligence.

- Surround yourself. The wealth mindset is influenced by the people, the surroundings, and the culture that you surround yourself with. You need to surround yourself with good, supporting, and inspiring people, who share your values, ambitions, and vision, and who can help you grow, challenge, and motivate you. You also need to surround yourself with a favorable, comfortable, and appealing environment that reflects your identity, personality, and lifestyle, and that can help you focus, relax, and enjoy. You also need to surround yourself with a wealth-oriented, success-oriented, and happiness-oriented society that can help you adopt, maintain, and keep the wealth mindset. You can use sources like media, events, communities, or role models, to assist you in immersing and exposing yourself to the wealth mindset.

- Challenge yourself. The wealth mindset is built on action, experience, and outcomes, that can help you build and attract riches and happiness in your life. You need to challenge yourself to take action, to try new things, and to attain your goals. You need to challenge yourself to move out of your comfort zone, to face your fears, and to overcome your hurdles. You need to challenge yourself to learn from your failures, to appreciate your victories, and to enhance your performance. You can utilize tools such as feedback, accountability, or coaching, to help you challenge and support yourself.

- Reward yourself. The prosperity mindset is focused on enjoyment, satisfaction, and fulfillment, which can help you produce and attract money and happiness in your life. You need to reward yourself for your efforts, your achievements, and your progress. You need to reward yourself with things that make you joyful, such as hobbies, passions, or experiences. You need to reward yourself with things that make you wealthy, such as investments, assets, or income. You need to reward yourself with things that make you healthy, such as rest, relaxation, or well-being. You can utilize methods like budgeting, planning, or tracking, to help you reward and balance yourself.

By following these strategies, you may nurture the wealth mindset, and use it to attain your financial goals and live your dream life.

Conclusion

The wealth mindset is the mindset of the wealthy, the successful, and the joyful. The riches mindset is focused on plenty, confidence, and possibilities. The wealth mindset is the mindset that helps us to create and attract wealth and happiness in our lives.

The poverty mindset is the mindset of the poor, the suffering, and the unhappy. The poor mindset is founded on fear, scarcity, and limitation. The poverty mindset is the thinking that inhibits us from creating and attracting riches and pleasure in our lives.

If we wish to overcome the poverty mindset and embrace the wealth mindset, we need to overcome fear, scarcity, and limiting ideas, that hold us back from producing and attracting prosperity and pleasure in our lives. We also need to build the wealth mindset, by educating ourselves, surrounding ourselves, challenging ourselves, and rewarding ourselves.

The wealth mindset is not something that we are born with, that we can buy, or that we can receive from someone else. The wealth mindset is something that we can build, cultivate, and grow, by ourselves, for ourselves, and with ourselves. The wealth mindset is a talent, a habit, and a decision, that we can learn, practice, and make, every day, in every scenario, and in every element of our lives.

The wealth mindset is the secret to building wealth and happiness, and it can be your key too.

Chapter 6

The Wealth Strategy

How to Plan, Execute, and Monitor Your Financial Goals

Having a wealth mindset is vital for building wealth and happiness, but it is not enough. You also need a wealth plan, a systematic and practical way to reach your financial goals and enjoy your dream life. A wealth strategy is a plan, a blueprint, and a roadmap, that leads your activities, decisions, and behaviors, towards creating and attracting money and pleasure in your life.

A wealth strategy is not a one-size-fits-all solution, nor is it a set of rules or formulas that you may blindly follow or copy from someone else. A wealth strategy is a specific and tailored solution, that reflects your beliefs, vision, and situation, and that you can alter and modify according to your needs, preferences, and circumstances. A wealth strategy is not a static or permanent answer, but a dynamic and flexible one, that changes and improves as you learn, grow, and change.

In this chapter, we will cover the three key components of a wealth strategy: planning, executing, and monitoring. We will also learn how to build, implement, and assess your own wealth plan, and how to use it to attain your financial goals and live your ideal life.

Planning

Planning is the first and most crucial component of a wealth plan. Planning is the process of identifying your financial goals, reviewing your existing status, and designing your action plan. Planning is the cornerstone of your wealth strategy, and it dictates the direction, scale, and quality of your money production and attraction.

Planning covers three basic steps: goal-setting, scenario analysis, and action design.

Goal-setting

Goal-setting is the process of identifying and clarifying your financial goals and making them explicit, measurable, realistic, relevant, and time-bound. Goal-setting is the starting point of your wealth strategy, and it sets the destination, purpose, and motivation of your wealth generation and attraction.

Goal-setting includes addressing three basic questions: what, why, and when.

- What: What are your financial goals? What do you want to achieve, generate, or attract, in terms of money, prosperity, and happiness? What are the outcomes, results, or signs that you desire to see, feel, or experience, in your financial life?

- Why: Why are your financial goals important to you? Why do you want to attain, generate, or attract your financial goals? Why are your financial goals associated with your values, vision, and mission, in your personal and professional life?

- When: When do you wish to attain, generate, or attract your financial goals? When are your deadlines, milestones, or checkpoints, for your financial goals? When are you planning to start, finish, or reassess your financial goals?

Goal-setting needs you to be clear, practical, and ambitious, about your financial goals. You need to be clear about what you want, why you want it, and when you want it, and avoid unclear, ambiguous, or contradicting goals. You need to be realistic about what you can achieve, create, or attract, and avoid unattainable, unreasonable, or unrealistic aspirations. You need to be ambitious about what you want to achieve, produce, or attract, and avoid easy, simple, or mediocre aims.

Goal-setting also needs you to write down, picture, and reinforce your financial goals. You need to write down your financial goals, in a clear, simple, and positive way, and maintain them in a visible, accessible, and remembered area. You need to visualize your financial goals, in a vivid, detailed, and emotional way, and imagine yourself attaining, producing, or attracting your financial goals. You need to restate your financial goals, in a confident, optimistic, and empowering way, and repeat them to yourself every day, or whenever you need a burst of motivation or inspiration.

Goal-setting is the first step in designing your wealth strategy, and it helps you to produce and attract money and happiness in your life.

Situation Analysis

Condition analysis is the process of examining and comprehending your current financial condition, and determining your strengths, weaknesses, opportunities, and dangers. Situation analysis is the second part of developing your wealth strategy, and it determines the starting place, the realities, and the problems of your money production and attraction. Situation analysis requires addressing four main questions: where, how, who, and what.

- Where: Where are you presently, in terms of your financial situation? Where are your present income, expenses, assets, liabilities, cash flow, and net worth? Where are your current sources, streams, and levels of income and wealth?

- How: How did you get to where you are now, in terms of your financial situation? How did your prior choices, actions, and behaviors affect your current financial situation? How did your past experiences, influences, and education, shape your current financial situation?

- Who: Who are the people that are involved in your financial situation? Who are your family, friends, partners, mentors, or advisers, that support, assist, or influence, your financial situation? Who are your competitors, enemies, or detractors, that challenge, obstruct, or endanger your financial situation?

- **What:** What are the things that affect your financial situation? What are the internal variables, such as your talents, knowledge, habits, or mindset, that affect your financial situation? What are the external elements, such as the economy, the market, the industry, or the society, that affect your financial situation?

Status analysis needs you to be honest, objective, and detailed, about your financial status. You need to be honest about your current financial status and avoid denial, distortion, or dishonesty. You need to be impartial about your current financial status, and avoid bias, emotion, or judgment. You need to be detailed about your current financial condition and avoid omission, exclusion, or generalization.

Situation analysis also demands you to acquire, arrange, and analyze your financial data. You need to collect your financial data, such as your revenue statements, expense reports, balance sheets, cash flow statements, and net worth statements, and keep them in a secure, accurate, and updated fashion. You need to arrange your financial data, such as by categorizing, labeling, or sorting, your financial data, and store them in a clear, straightforward, and consistent fashion. You need to evaluate your financial data, such as by calculating, comparing, or assessing your financial statistics, and keep them in a meaningful, usable, and actionable way.

status analysis is the second part of developing your wealth strategy, and it enables you to understand and improve your financial status.

Action Design

Action design is the process of designing and preparing your action plan, and selecting what, how, and when, you are going to do, to reach your financial goals. Action design is the third part of developing your wealth strategy, and it dictates the course, method, and quality of your wealth production and attraction.

Action design includes answering three basic questions: what, how, and when.

- What: What are the actions that you are going to do, to reach your financial goals? What are the actions, activities, or steps that you are going to undertake, to create or attract money, wealth, and happiness, in your life?

- How: How are you going to take the actions to reach your financial goals? How are you going to execute, implement, or accomplish, your tasks, actions, or steps, to create or attract money, riches, and happiness, in your life?

- When: When are you going to take the actions to attain your financial goals? When are your deadlines, milestones, or checkpoints, for your duties, activities, or steps, to create or attract money, riches, and happiness, in your life?

Action design requires you to be clear, realistic, and ambitious, about your actions. You need to be explicit about what you are going to do, how you are going to do it, and when you are going to do it and avoid vague, ambiguous, or conflicting acts. You need to be realistic about what you can do, how you can do it, and when you can do it, and avoid impossible, impractical, or unrealistic acts. You need to be ambitious about what you want to accomplish, how you want to do it, and when you want to do it and reject easy, simple, or mediocre acts.

Action design also needs you to prioritize, schedule, and commit to your actions. You need to prioritize your actions, by ranking, ordering, or filtering your actions according to their importance, urgency, or impact, and focus on the most crucial, essential, or valuable acts. You need to schedule your actions, by allocating, assigning, or distributing, your time, energy, and resources, to your actions, according to their duration, frequency, or intensity, and plan ahead, prepare, or arrange your actions. You need to commit to your actions, by deciding, vowing, or pledging, to take your actions, regardless of the hurdles, problems, or distractions, and follow through, persist, or stick to your actions.

Action design is the third part of developing your wealth strategy, and it allows you to create and attract money and happiness in your life.

Executing

Executing is the second and most challenging component of a wealth plan. Executing is the process of taking action, implementing your action plan, and doing what you need to do, to reach your financial goals. Executing is the core of your wealth plan, and it defines the speed, efficiency, and efficacy of your money production and attraction.

Executing requires three primary steps: action-taking, problem-solving, and result-producing.

Action-taking

Action-taking is the step where you really implement the steps that you have outlined in your wealth strategy. For example, if your strategy involves saving a certain amount of money every month, then you need to set up a mechanism that automatically sends that amount from your paycheck to your savings account. Action-taking is the most critical step since it is where you put your intentions into reality. However, action-taking also comes with problems and hurdles that you need to overcome.

- Problem-solving: This is the step when you identify and resolve the challenges that develop during your action-taking. For example, if your income changes or drops, then you need to discover a means to adapt your savings plan accordingly. Problem-solving is the step where you utilize your creativity and resourcefulness to create solutions that work for you. Problem-solving is vital since it helps you to stay on track and avoid giving up on your wealth strategy.

- Result-producing: This is the step when you assess and evaluate the outcomes of your action-taking and problem-solving. For example, if your aim is to build a certain amount of wealth in a given time frame, then you need to track your progress and compare it with your target. Result-producing is the step where you use feedback and data to assess your performance and make adjustments. Result-producing is vital since it helps you to see the results of your work and celebrate your achievements.

The nest egg myth

Chapter 7

The Wealth Habits

How to Develop the Skills, Knowledge, and Discipline to Achieve Financial Freedom

In this chapter, you will learn how to establish the habits that will assist you in building money and happiness outside of the traditional system. You will uncover the four fundamental behaviors that successful wealth builders have in common, and how you may adopt them in your own life. These habits are:

- Learning: How to obtain the skills and knowledge that will raise your worth and income in the market.
- Earning: How to develop several streams of revenue from your abilities, knowledge, and assets.
- Saving: How to manage your spending and save a large percentage of your income for investment.

- Investing: How to enhance your money by investing in assets that create passive income and appreciate over time.

By mastering these habits, you will be able to construct a sustainable and scalable wealth strategy that will allow you to attain financial freedom and live the life you want. You will also be able to avoid the flaws and risks of the conventional system, such as relying on a single source of income, saving in low-interest accounts, and investing in volatile and speculative markets.

Let's start with the first habit: learning.

Learning: How to obtain the skills and knowledge that will raise your worth and income in the market.

Learning is the foundation of wealth growth. Without studying, you will not be able to gain the skills and information that will make you useful and in demand in the market. Learning will also assist you in adapting to the changing requirements and opportunities of the economy and identifying new methods to create value and revenue for yourself and others.

Learning is not something that you do exclusively at school or college. Learning is a lifelong process that involves curiosity, dedication, and tenacity. You should continually be looking for ways to improve your existing talents, gain new skills, and broaden your knowledge base. You should also be open to comments and
criticism, and eager to learn from your mistakes and shortcomings.

There are various ways to learn, such as reading books, taking classes, watching videos, listening to podcasts, attending seminars, joining communities, finding mentors, and executing projects. You should choose the approaches that suit your learning style, goals, and budget. You should also vary your learning sources, and avoid relying on a single authority or platform.

The key to effective learning is to apply what you learn. Learning without action is useless. You should always look for opportunities to employ your skills and knowledge in real-world circumstances, such as your work, your business, your hobbies, or your social causes. This will assist you to test your comprehension, gain experience, and produce value. It will also enable you to recognize your strengths and limitations and to pinpoint opportunities for progress.

Learning is not only useful for your wealth but also for your happiness. Learning may enrich your life, stimulate your intellect, challenge your limits, and extend your horizons. Learning can also provide you with a sense of purpose, achievement, and fulfillment. Learning may make you a better person, and a better wealth builder.

Earning: How to develop various sources of income from your abilities, expertise, and assets, and how to improve your income by adding value, solving issues, and generating solutions.

Earning is the second habit of wealth creation. Without income, you would not be able to save and invest your money to develop your wealth. Earning is also a way to show your value, contribute to the world and enjoy the results of your labor.

Earning is not something that you do solely in a job or a career. Earning is an attitude that attempts to develop various streams of revenue from your abilities, knowledge, and assets. Multiple streams of income can provide you with more security, flexibility, and possibilities to enhance your wealth. Multiple streams of income might also enable you to attain financial freedom sooner, as you will not be dependent on a single source of money.

There are various ways to establish several streams of income, such as founding a business, freelancing, consulting, coaching, teaching, developing products, selling services, licensing your ideas, renting your assets, or investing in income-generating assets. You should choose the methods that suit your talents, knowledge, and interests. You should also diversify your income sources, and avoid relying on a single client, customer, or market.

The key to effective earning is to raise your income by adding value, addressing problems, and generating solutions. Adding value is delivering anything that is useful, valuable, or attractive to others. Solving problems entails finding and fixing the pain areas, obstacles, or needs of others. Creating solutions implies designing and delivering the items, services, or systems that can satisfy the value or problem of others.

You can improve your income by offering value, solving problems, and generating solutions in several ways, such as enhancing your quality, speed, or efficiency, expanding your scope, scale, or reach, inventing your design, features, or functionalities, or differentiating your brand, style, or story. You can also improve your income by negotiating your rates, fees, or pricing, or by generating passive or residual income sources that require less time, effort, or maintenance.

There are many examples of successful entrepreneurs, freelancers, and investors who have developed several streams of income and grown their income by adding value, solving problems, and generating solutions. For instance, **Elon Musk** is an entrepreneur who has started and operated many businesses in diverse industries, such as PayPal, SpaceX, Tesla, SolarCity, and Neuralink. He has also enhanced his revenue by proposing new and visionary ideas for the future of payments, space exploration, transportation, energy, and brain-computer interfaces. Another example is **Tim Ferriss**, a freelancer who has developed many sources of income from his abilities and experience in various industries, such as writing, podcasting, investing, consulting, and teaching. He has also boosted his income by adding value and solving problems for millions of individuals who want to learn how to live a better, smarter, and richer life. A third example is **Warren Buffett**, an investor who has amassed vast wealth by investing in many assets, such as stocks, bonds, real estate, and enterprises. He has also grown his income by following his concepts of value investing, which focus on locating and buying undervalued and high-quality assets that may create constant and growing income over time.

By following these examples, you may also develop several streams of income and improve your income by adding value, solving problems, and creating solutions. This will assist you to earn more money, and to generate greater riches and happiness. Earning is not only useful for your wealth but also for your fulfillment. Earning can provide you with a sense of achievement, acknowledgment, and satisfaction. Earning can make you a better person, and a greater money builder.

Saving: How to control your expenses and save a high percentage of your income for investment, and how to develop a budget, track your spending, and cut your costs.

Saving is the third habit of wealth growth. Without saving, you would not be able to invest your money to expand your fortune. Saving is also a method to safeguard your wealth plan for the future and to enjoy the independence and peace of mind that come from having a financial cushion.

Saving is not something that you do simply when you have extra money or when you want to buy something. Saving is an attitude that aims to manage your spending and save a large percentage of your income for investing. A high percentage of income can be anything from 10% to 50% or more, depending on your goals and circumstances. Saving a high proportion of income can allow you to attain financial freedom sooner since you will be able to invest more money and compound your gains faster.

There are various ways to control your expenses and save a large percentage of your income for investment, such as making a budget, tracking your spending, and reducing your costs. Creating a budget implies placing a limit on how much you can spend on different categories, such as accommodation, food, transportation, entertainment, etc. Tracking your expenditure includes recording and assessing how much you actually spend on each category, and comparing it with your budget. Reducing your expenditures includes finding and eliminating the unneeded, wasteful, or excessive spending that does not bring value to your life, and finding ways to cut your expenses on the essential or desirable spending that does add value to your life.

You can construct a budget, track your spending, and minimize your costs in numerous methods, such as using apps, tools, or spreadsheets, following the 50/30/20 rule, applying the zero-based budgeting strategy, or using the envelope system. You can also employ tips and methods, like paying yourself first, automating your savings, utilizing cash instead of credit cards, or using the 30-day rule. You should choose the ways that suit your interests, habits, and lifestyle. You should also examine and change your budget, spending, and costs often, and applaud your progress and achievements.

There are many examples of frugal millionaires, minimalists, and savers who have managed their spending, saved a large percentage of their income for investing, and attained financial freedom by living below their means and saving aggressively. For instance, **Warren Buffett** is a frugal millionaire who lives in the same humble house he bought in 1958, drives an ordinary automobile, and spends less than $4 on breakfast. He has also saved and invested a considerable percentage of his salary and accumulated a fortune of over $100 billion. Another example is **Joshua Fields Millburn and Ryan Nicodemus**, often known as The Minimalists, who are minimalists who have reduced their possessions, expenses, and stress, and improved their pleasure, freedom, and significance. They have also saved and invested a large amount of their income and achieved financial independence in their 30s. A third example is **Mr. Money Mustache**, a saver who retired at the age of 30 by living on less than $25,000 a year, saving over 65% of his salary, and investing in low-cost index funds. He has also influenced millions of people to embrace his philosophy of frugality, simplicity, and happiness.

By following these examples, you may also limit your spending, save a large percentage of your salary for investing, and attain financial freedom by living below your means and saving aggressively. This will assist you to save more money, and to build more wealth and security. Saving is not only excellent for your wealth, but also for your well-being. Saving can offer you a sense of control, confidence, and calmness. Saving may make you a better person, and a better money builder.

Investing

Investing is one of the best methods to enhance your wealth over time. By investing in assets that produce passive income and appreciate in value, you may establish a constant source of cash flow and enhance your net worth. However, investment is not a get-rich-quick plan. It demands patience, discipline, knowledge, and strategy. Here are some advice on how to invest effectively and grow wealth:

- Choose the correct investments. There are various sorts of investments, such as stocks, bonds, real estate, commodities, cryptocurrency, etc. Each one has its own risk-reward profile, liquidity, volatility, and tax consequences. You should conduct your homework and grasp the pros and cons of each investment before putting your money into it. You should also examine your goals, time horizon, risk tolerance, and personal preferences when choosing your assets.
- Diversify your assets. Diversification involves distributing your money over numerous sorts of investments, sectors,

companies, regions, and asset classes. In this manner, you may limit your exposure to any particular risk element and boost your chances of earning higher profits. Diversification also helps you cope with market changes and minimize emotional reactions to price movements. You should diversify your portfolio according to your risk appetite and investing objectives.

- Compound your returns. Compounding implies reinvesting your earnings back into your investments so that you can receive interest on interest. In this manner, you can accelerate the growth of your wealth and reach exponential returns over time. Compounding is one of the most powerful forces in investing, as it can turn modest amounts of money into big sums over the long run. You should take advantage of compounding by reinvesting your dividends, interest, capital gains, and other income sources into your portfolio.

- Learn from successful investors, traders, and company owners. There are many examples of people who have acquired money by investing intelligently and strategically. Some of them are Warren Buffett, the legendary investor who is known for his value investing philosophy and long-term approach; George Soros, the billionaire hedge fund manager who is famous for his currency trading and macroeconomic analysis; Jeff Bezos, the founder and CEO of Amazon, who is the richest person in the world and has revolutionized e-commerce and cloud computing; and Elon Musk, the visionary entrepreneur who is the founder and CEO of Tesla, SpaceX, and Neuralink, and has disrupted the automotive, aerospace, and biotechnology industries. You can learn from their tales, thoughts, techniques, and concepts, and apply them to your own investment path.

The nest egg myth

Chapter 8

The Wealth Lifestyle

How to Enjoy Your Money and Live a Fulfilling Life

Many people think that the ultimate purpose of investing is to accumulate a huge nest egg that will allow them to retire comfortably and securely. However, this is a fallacy that can lead to dissatisfaction, tension, and unhappiness. In this chapter, we will show you how to appreciate your money and live a meaningful life, regardless of how much you have in your bank account.

The first step to living a wealthy lifestyle is to define what money means to you. Wealth is not just a number, but a state of mind and a way of living. Wealth is about having enough money to meet your necessities and wants, but also having enough time, freedom, choice, and happiness to follow your interests and purpose. Wealth is about producing value for yourself and others and having a positive effect on the world.

The second stage to creating a prosperous lifestyle is to connect your spending with your values and priorities. Many people waste money on things that do not bring them joy or happiness, such as superfluous expenses, impulse purchases, or keeping up with the Joneses. Instead, you should spend money on things that matter to you, such as experiences, education, health, relationships, or causes. You should also save and invest money for your future aspirations, such as traveling, starting a business, or leaving a legacy.

The third step to establishing a prosperous lifestyle is to optimize your income and spending. You can boost your income by increasing your talents, expanding your network, producing numerous streams of income, or launching a side hustle. You may lower your expenses by budgeting, tracking, and cutting down on unneeded or excessive spending. You can also employ tactics such as automation, negotiation, or tax optimization to save more money and develop your wealth faster.

The fourth stage to having a rich lifestyle is to adopt a wealthy mindset. A wealth mindset is a combination of beliefs and attitudes that help you to attract and create riches in your life. A wealth mindset is built on the following principles:

- You are worthy of money and deserve to be prosperous.
- You have the power and obligation to build your own wealth and happiness.
- You have an abundant mentality and see opportunities everywhere.
- You are appreciative of what you have and generous with what you share.
- You are hopeful and confident about your future and potential.
- You possess a curious mentality, demonstrating a tremendous drive to study and improve.
- You are robust and adaptive to change and obstacles.

The fifth and last stage to living a prosperous lifestyle is to enjoy the trip and celebrate your achievements. Many people postpone their happiness until they attain a particular level of income or success, but this is a mistake. You should enjoy the process of building riches and happiness, and embrace every moment and milestone along the road. It's essential to acknowledge and commemorate your accomplishments, taking the time to recognize the fruits of your labor and rewarding yourself for the effort and advancements you've made. You should also share your riches and happiness with others, and motivate others to live a prosperous lifestyle as well.

By following these methods, you can live a rich lifestyle that is not based on the size of your nest egg, but on the quality of your life. You can enjoy your money and live a meaningful life, while also accumulating wealth and happiness outside of the usual system. You may break free from the nest egg fallacy, and establish your own prosperity reality.

Chapter 9

The Wealth Legacy

How to Protect, Grow, and Share Your Wealth with Future Generations

Wealth legacy is the idea of leaving behind something useful and meaningful for future generations. It is not just about how much money you have, but also about what you do with it and how you pass it on. Wealth legacy is crucial for those who wish to generate wealth and pleasure outside of the regular system because it allows them to:

- Preserve their hard-earned wealth and defend it from external risks such as taxes, inflation, lawsuits, and creditors.
- Grow their money and make it work for them and their family, by investing sensibly, diversifying their portfolio, and taking advantage of compound interest.
- Share their riches and make a positive impact on the world, by supporting organizations

they care about, generating opportunities for others, and leaving a lasting legacy of giving and kindness.

- Transfer their wealth and teach their heirs how to handle it safely, by giving them financial education, mentoring, and assistance.
- Transmit their wealth and inculcate their beliefs, skills, knowledge, and vision in their future generations, by setting an example, sharing their tales, and inspiring them to chase their aspirations.

Wealth legacy is not just about money, but also about values, skills, knowledge, and effects that you may pass on to your future generations. By creating a financial legacy, you may ensure that your riches and happiness will survive beyond your lifetime and that you will leave the world a better place than you found it.

Some of the common obstacles and pitfalls that people confront when seeking to safeguard, grow, and share their money with their heirs are:

- Taxes: Taxes can diminish the amount of money that you can pass on to your heirs, especially if you do not prepare ahead and employ measures such as trusts, gifts, and charitable donations to minimize your tax liability. According to a survey by Wealth-X, the global average effective inheritance tax rate is 16.7%, however, it can vary substantially depending on the jurisdiction and the size of the estate.

- Inflation: Inflation can reduce the purchasing power of your wealth over time, especially if you do not invest your money in assets that can stay up with or beat inflation. According to the World Bank, the global average inflation rate was 3.2% in 2021, but it might fluctuate based on the economic situation and the monetary policies of individual countries.

- Lawsuits: Lawsuits might expose your wealth to legal dangers, especially if you are involved in a business, a profession, or an activity that can attract litigation. According to research by the Pacific Research Institute, the yearly direct cost of the U.S. tort system was $429 billion in 2016, which is equal to 2.3% of the U.S. gross domestic product.

- **Family problems:** Family conflicts might emerge when you try to transfer your fortune among your successors, especially if you do not convey your objectives clearly and properly. According to a survey by TD Wealth, 44% of estate planning professionals claimed that family conflicts were the largest threat to estate planning in 2019, and the most prevalent cause of disagreement was the selection of beneficiaries.

- **Lack of financial literacy:** Lack of financial literacy might prohibit your successors from managing your wealth responsibly, especially if they do not have the information, skills, and confidence to make informed financial decisions. According to a survey by the Organisation for Economic Co-operation and Development, just 38% of individuals in 31 countries acquired the basic level of financial literacy in 2018.

- **Irresponsible spending:** Irresponsible spending can deplete your fortune quickly, especially if your heirs do not have the discipline, budgeting, and saving skills to live within their means. According to research by Ohio State University, one-third of Americans who receive an inheritance have negative savings within two years of acquiring their money.

These are some of the usual obstacles and pitfalls that people confront when seeking to safeguard, grow, and share their fortune with their heirs. You can avoid or overcome these issues by planning ahead, seeking professional counsel, educating your heirs, and setting clear expectations and boundaries. By doing so, you can build a wealth legacy that will continue for decades.

Some of the practical tactics and recommendations on how to overcome these problems and produce a lasting wealth legacy are:

- Estate planning: Estate planning is the act of structuring your affairs and assets in a way that will ensure your desires are carried out after your death. Estate planning can help you avoid probate, cut taxes, safeguard your possessions, and provide for your loved ones. Some of the steps involved in estate planning are making a will, naming beneficiaries, selecting executors, and setting up trusts.

- Trusts: Trusts are legal structures that allow you to transfer your assets to a trustee, who will manage them according to your instructions for the benefit of your beneficiaries. Trusts can help you secure your assets from creditors, lawsuits, and taxes, as well as govern how and when your heirs receive their inheritance. Some of the forms of trusts are revocable trusts, irrevocable trusts, living trusts, and testamentary trusts.

- **Wills:** Wills are legal papers that indicate how you want your property and affairs to be handled after your death. Wills can help you divide your assets according to your intentions, name guardians for your minor children, and designate charity donations. Some of the elements of a will are the testator, the beneficiaries, the executor, the witnesses, and the signature.

- **Life insurance:** Life insurance is a contract between you and an insurance company, where you pay a premium in exchange for a death benefit that will be paid to your dependents upon your death. Life insurance can help you provide financial security for your family, cover your bills and expenses, and generate a tax-free estate. Some of the types of life insurance are term life insurance, whole life insurance, universal life insurance, and variable life insurance.

- **Charitable giving:** Charitable giving is the act of providing money or assets to a cause or organization that you care about. Charitable giving can help you promote your ideals, make a beneficial impact on the world, and reduce your taxes. Some of the means of charitable giving are direct donations, donor-advised funds, charitable trusts, and foundations.

- **Investing:** Investing is the process of placing your money into assets that can provide income or appreciate in value over time. Investing can help you grow your wealth, fight inflation, and achieve your financial goals. Some of the sorts of investments are equities, bonds, mutual funds, exchange-traded funds, real estate, and cryptocurrencies.

- **Education:** Education is the process of learning knowledge, skills, and abilities that can help you enhance your life and career. Education can help you boost your income, extend your options, and promote your well-being. Some of the forms of education are formal education, informal education, self-education, and lifelong learning.

- **Mentoring:** Mentoring is the relationship between a mentor and a mentee, where the mentor provides direction, support, and feedback to the mentee. Mentoring may help you pass on your wisdom, experience, and values to your future generations, as well as inspire them to follow their goals and dreams. Some of the characteristics of mentoring are setting expectations, creating trust, sharing tales, and giving advice.

These are some of the practical strategies and tips on how to overcome these problems and create a lasting wealth legacy. By implementing these tactics, you may ensure that your money and enjoyment will be preserved, enhanced, and shared with your future generations.

- **Warren Buffett:** The famed investor and philanthropist has vowed to give away more than 99% of his fortune to charity causes, largely through the *Bill & Melinda Gates Foundation*. He has also inspired other billionaires to sign the *Giving Pledge*, a vow to contribute at least half of their money to charity. Buffett believes that his riches should be utilized to better the lives of others, not to create dynasties or perpetuate inequality. He expressed the sentiment, 'I aspire to provide my children with sufficient support to instill in them the belief that they can achieve anything, yet not to the extent that it fosters a sense of complacency."

- **Oprah Winfrey:** The media mogul and entrepreneur has used her riches and influence to assist different causes, such as education, women's empowerment, health, and human rights. She has donated millions of dollars to numerous organizations, such as the *Oprah Winfrey Leadership Academy for Girls* in South Africa, the *Angel Network,* and the *Oprah Winfrey Foundation.* She has also founded her own television network, *OWN,* which creates material that inspires and uplifts people. Winfrey thinks that her riches are a means to serve others, not to gain more. She previously claimed, "The reason I've been able to be so financially successful is my focus has never, ever for one minute been money."

- **Azim Premji:** The Indian billionaire and founder of **Wipro**, one of the greatest IT businesses in the world, has donated more than half of his wealth to his foundation, *the Azim*

Premji Foundation strives to improve the quality and equity of education in India. He has also sponsored various efforts, such as health, nutrition, and rural development. Premji feels that his money is a social responsibility, not a personal privilege. He has expressed before, "I firmly endorse the idea that individuals fortunate enough to possess wealth ought to make substantial contributions to actively foster a more improved world for the millions facing considerably fewer privileges."

These are only a few of the examples of those who have built a rich legacy that goes beyond their own lives. They have used their riches to promote causes they care about, to provide opportunities for others, and to make a positive difference in the world.

I hope you find these inspiring and motivational.

The nest egg myth

The nest egg myth

About the Author

Meet John S. Mathis, a visionary author and financial maverick who has committed his life to unraveling the accepted rules surrounding wealth and happiness. With a bright intellect and a desire to challenge the existing quo, Jesse brings a novel viewpoint to the world of finance.

Armed with a varied background in economics, psychology, and alternative investment tactics, John S. Mathis is not your usual financial expert. His journey into the field of unconventional wealth-building began when he questioned the age-old notion of the "nest egg" — a term that he says inhibits our knowledge of actual riches.

John's writing is a blend of insightful research, practical guidance, and a dash of rebellious flair. In "The Nest Egg Myth," he masterfully navigates through the complexity of the old financial system, offering readers a blueprint to acquire money and achieve genuine happiness beyond its limitations.

Beyond his creative activities, John is a sought-after speaker known for his ability to fascinate audiences with his unusual wisdom. Whether examining economic ideas or sharing personal experiences, he leaves an unforgettable impact on the minds of people seeking a revolutionary approach to their financial path.

In a world overloaded with financial noise, John S. Mathis stands out as a light of clarity, pointing readers toward a future where financial prosperity and joy are not mutually contradictory. Join him on this transforming journey as he tackles the beliefs that constrain our notion of money and happiness.

"The Nest Egg Myth" is not simply a book; it's a manifesto for individuals eager to break free from the confines of conventional financial thinking. John S. Mathis urges you to embark on a road of empowerment, where money is redefined, and happiness is discovered in the unorthodox. Get ready to confront the myths, rewrite the rules, and create your individual route to prosperity